NEVER SAY DIE

The Story of Gladys Aylward

by
CYRIL DAVEY

LUTTERWORTH PRESS

LONDON

PRINTED IN GREAT BRITAIN
BY EBENEZER BAYLIS AND SON, LTD.
THE TRINITY PRESS, WORCESTER, AND LONDON

CONTENTS

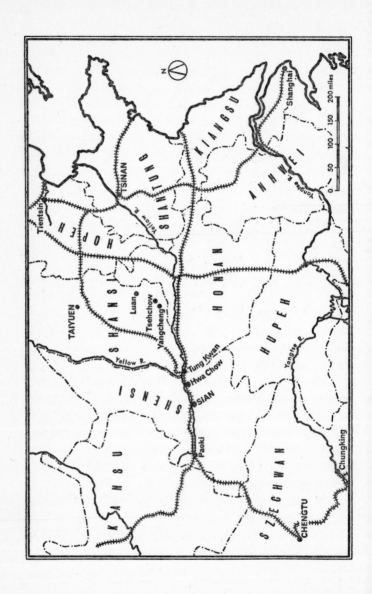

1

THE LITTLE PARLOURMAID

GLADYS sat very straight on the hard chair, waiting for the bad news which she knew she was going to hear. On the opposite side of the big desk she saw a thin-faced man who was trying his best to look kindly at her.

"It's no use trying to break it gently," she said, her misery making her voice sound sharp. "You're going to tell me I'm no good, aren't you?"

"Well . . . not exactly. I'm sure you'll find *something* you can do. There are lots of jobs in England where you can help our missionary work. There's a couple of retired missionaries just back from China who need someone to look after them, for instance. You were a parlourmaid before you came here, weren't you?"

Gladys felt as if she would break into tears. Instead, she almost snapped back. "I don't want to look after missionaries who've come back from China. I want to go to China myself!" Then, ashamed of herself, she spoke more quietly. "But all these exams and things . . . I'm not used to them. I wasn't ever much good at school. I told you that when I came to the College."

The principal of the China Inland Mission Training School leaned forward on the desk.

"I know it's a terrible disappointment, Gladys," he said gently, "but it's like this. You're twenty-six years old . . ."

"And only five feet high and I wasn't clever at school. My father was a postman and I had to help to look after the other children when I came home. I never had any chance to study at home and I didn't think it mattered anyway. I was only going to be a servant. But then, somehow, God seemed to be saying to me that He wanted me to go to China. I told you, I couldn't ever get rid of the feeling. Why should I feel like that if God didn't want me in China after all?"

"I don't know, Gladys. But we've done our best to help. We took you for three months' trial at the College. We don't worry too much about passing exams or what sort of schooling you had. But, if you stayed here for three years—and you'd have to do that—and then went to China, you'd be thirty. *And we know that anyone over thirty isn't ever likely to be able to learn the Chinese language properly!* That's the real trouble. We just don't feel we can keep you if . . ." His voice trailed off.

"If I'm going to be a failure when I get there," supplied Gladys. "I expect you're right." She smiled, ruefully. "Certainly you've done your best with me!"

"What will you do now?" asked the principal as she got up to leave the room.

"I don't know," she answered. But, as she closed the door, Gladys Aylward's face showed stubborn lines and there was a far-away look in her eyes. If the man at the desk had heard what she muttered to herself he would have been surprised. "I don't know what I'm going to do *now*—that's true. But I know what I'm going to do in the end. *I'm going to China!*"

It did look as if the principal was right. She had to admit that. She was an ordinary London girl without much education and she had no money. None of the missionary societies would accept her—not even the China Inland Mission which she had been so sure about. She'd tried doing welfare work at the Cardiff docks and most of the tough, drunken sailors had just laughed at her. She would never make a preacher, and she couldn't pass the exams to be a nurse even if she tried. No. They were probably right. She would have to get a job as a servant again.

The employment agency gave her an address—a big house in London belonging to a famous explorer, Sir Francis Younghusband—and she was quickly taken on as a parlourmaid. Her employer, who had made exploring journeys across China, and the principal of the training college she had left, would have been very surprised if they had seen what she did when she unpacked her tiny bag in her new attic-room.

She took out her Bible, laid it on the table by her bed, opened her purse and took out all the money she had left. There were two pennies and a halfpenny. She laid them on her Bible.

"Oh, God!" she said. "Here's my Bible. Here's my money. Here's me. Please use me—in China!"

An hour later she had three shillings and twopence halfpenny because the housekeeper had paid back her fare. She added the three shillings to the money on her Bible and smiled happily to herself.

If anyone had asked Gladys about China she would not have been able to tell them much. To her, the most important thing was that most of its millions of people

9

knew nothing about Jesus and she wanted to tell them about Him. What part of China she wanted to go to, she had no idea. That would settle itself when the time came, she felt sure. And as for learning the language . . . This time she did not smile at all. The college might be right. She felt sure she would never be able to understand the queer, ornamental letters the Chinese used, or read down the page instead of across it. But surely, she felt, if you lived with people you would gradually begin to understand what they were talking about? For the time being, she gave up worrying about the future. The important matter was to save enough money to pay her fare, and how much that might be she had no idea.

* * *

A little while later she found out.

At a travel-agency in the Haymarket, in London, she asked the clerk behind the counter.

"China, madam?" He looked in surprise at the five-foot, poorly-dressed young woman. "Yes, certainly. Do you want a ticket now?"

"Good gracious, no!" Gladys sounded horrified, clutching the three pounds in her hand. "I only wanted to inquire how much it costs."

"Ninety pounds single fare, madam."

Gladys looked as if she were going to faint. "Isn't there anything cheaper?"

"Not really, no. That's by ship, of course." He hesitated. "There's the railway—across Russia and Siberia. That costs forty-seven pounds ten shillings." As Gladys began to brighten he went on. "But you can't go that way,

I'm afraid. You see, madam, there's a war on between China and Russia." As Gladys prepared to say that *she* wasn't worried about a war, he went on. "They just don't take passengers any more. A lot of the railway has been bombed. It may be years before it's open again."

Gladys looked more cheerful. "Well, that's all right, then. It may be years before I can go, so perhaps the war will be over by then. You see, I want to be a missionary and I've got to save the fare. If I come in every week and give you something towards it will you keep it for me?"

The clerk hesitated. "We don't usually do things like that."

"Never mind. You can do it for me. It will be safer with you than in my drawer where I work. Here's the first three pounds." She almost laughed at the look on his face. "That means I've only got to save another forty-four pounds ten."

As she left the travel-agency she felt as if she were almost on the way to China already. She became even more certain of the future when some friends told her about Jeannie Lawson. Mrs. Lawson had been working on her own as a missionary, deep amongst the hills in the interior of China, and had written to say that she was getting old and needed someone to help her. She did not belong to any missionary society and, to Gladys, she sounded exactly the kind of person she would like to work with. She wrote at once.

★   ★   ★

It was months later when the postman brought a letter

addressed to Gladys Aylward to the big house in Belgrave Square. For months the other servants had regarded her as a bit "queer" with her talk of China. Now that a letter with a strange Chinese stamp lay on the mat they were not so sure.

Mrs. Lawson's letter was short and simple. She would be delighted to accept Gladys's offer of help. If she could find her own way to Tientsin Mrs. Lawson would see that she was met by a messenger who would guide her to her journey's end. Mrs. Lawson made it sound as if "getting to Tientsin" was as easy as taking a bus-ride down the road, but at first Gladys could hardly find the town on the map of Asia which she kept in her room.

When at last she put her finger on it she really did begin to wonder if she was as mad as the other servants in the house thought her. It was not only hundreds, but thousands, of miles away. She might possibly never see her home or her parents again. In spite of all the extra work she had done to earn more than her wages—working on her day off and at week-ends, serving at big dinners, walking instead of riding on the trams—she had still not quite saved her forty-seven pounds ten shillings. And, if she managed to save it and survive the long journey to China, it seemed that she would never be able to save enough to come home again. Nobody would be responsible for her when she got there and she would have no salary. If anything happened to the shadowy Jeannie Lawson she would be completely on her own. If that happened she would *have* to speak Chinese, whether the man at the training college thought she could learn it or not.

Gladys sat down on the uncomfortable chair in her

bedroom. "Am I quite crazy?" she asked herself. "Am I just being stubborn because everyone says I can't do it? Or has God really got something for me to do at the other side of the world?"

2

DANGEROUS JOURNEY

"ARE you sure you've got *everything*?"

It might have been a mother, father and sister seeing the other member of the family off for a holiday. At Liverpool Street station, in London, there were plenty of people doing the same thing. But that Saturday morning there was probably nobody on the train who was going so far, or would have such astonishing adventures, as the small, soberly-dressed woman who waved her last good-byes as the train slowly chugged out of the platform towards Harwich and the boat for Holland.

Nor, for that matter, was anyone else's luggage quite the same as hers. She had two suitcases. One was full of her clothes, the other was crammed with tins of soup, baked beans, biscuits, hard-boiled eggs, coffee and soda-cakes. To the handle of the suitcase were tied a kettle and a saucepan, and on the rack stood a little spirit-stove. Under her clothes she carried a Bible, her tickets, a passport, some writing-paper and a fountain pen. In her purse she had ninepence in coppers.

"After all," said Gladys Aylward to her fellow-passengers, "I don't quite know what I may need on the journey. I'm going to China."

The date was Saturday, October 18, 1930.

After crossing the North Sea she looked up and down

the train standing at The Hague, got into a corner seat and waited for the journey to begin that would take her across Holland, Germany, Poland, Russia and Manchuria.

"How long will it take me to get to China?" she asked the ticket-collector.

He understood English, but he looked at her as if he could not believe his ears. "Fourteen days," he answered, shrugging his shoulders. "Two weeks!" Gladys looked at her suitcase on the rack, and wondered if she had enough food for a fortnight. The man's next words made her sit up sharply. Perhaps the clerk in the travel-agency had been right after all. "You will not get there. There is a war! You may be killed . . . you may have to stay in Russia. But you will not get to China, Miss!" He punched her ticket, stared at her as if she was mad and went on down the train.

* * *

The long, slow journey dragged on. It was nearly a week after leaving The Hague that the train pulled into the main station in Moscow. Ten days had passed when they moved across the border into Siberia. Every now and again she unwrapped herself from the rug, made from a fur coat someone had given her mother, and tramped up the corridor, trying to keep warm. The food in her suitcase grew less and less. There was ice on the water buckets in the stations and sometimes the taps were frozen so that she could not get any water to boil her coffee. Everywhere she looked, deep snow stretched away towards the mountains. But, as she trudged up and down the train, she realized something else.

She was the only civilian on the whole train. There were no other women. And every man on the train was a soldier. The men stared at her but it was no use trying to talk to them. Not one of them could understand English. All they could do was make signs to her and shrug their shoulders. The signs were clear enough. They meant that, just ahead of them, war was raging.

When at last the train pulled into a station named Chita more and more soldiers piled on. A few hours later, in the darkness, it halted again and the soldiers lumbered out, grasping their packs and rifles, and disappeared into the darkness. Once more Gladys walked up the train, looking into every compartment.

She was quite alone. Not even the driver had stayed in the engine-cab. As she looked out into the dark night, clutching her clothes and her rug round her to get a little warmth in the howling gale that drove across the flat landscape, she saw a flash of light. Then another and another. In the distance something like thunder roared and rattled. But Gladys knew it was not thunder, nor were the flashes lightning. Everyone who had warned her had been right, after all.

There really was a war, here on the border-land of Russia and China. And Gladys Aylward, the parlourmaid who wanted to be a missionary, was just on the edge of it.

*   *   *

"Go back! Back to Chita!"

Someone, at any rate, was able to speak a little English and Gladys discovered a group of four men huddled round a fire—the driver, the stoker, the guard and the station-master. They told her the train would stay where it was for days, perhaps weeks, and then take the wounded back to hospital. To return to Chita was to turn her back on China, but there was nothing else to do. She could hardly walk through the two armies fighting on the border. Carrying her two suitcases, with the kettle and the saucepan banging against the side, she started to trudge down the railway-line, through dark tunnels, over the snowdrifts, until at last she could go no further. Putting her suitcases one on each side of her to keep off the bitter wind she dropped off to sleep. The last sound she heard was what she thought were howling dogs in the forests. Only much later did she discover that she had fallen asleep with the sound of a pack of hunting wolves in her ears.

Back at Chita, after walking most of the night and all day, she showed the police her passport and her Bible. They looked at the word "missionary" in the passport and exchanged sharp glances with each other; then, after long arguments which she could not understand, took her to an office, gave her new tickets and put her on a train.

"Nikolshissur," the police shouted. "Pogranilchnai!" Gladys shrugged her shoulders. She did not understand anything of what they said. The words might have meant anything at all. Only when they pointed to them in a railway time-table did she realize that they were towns to which the train was going. She had to change at the first of them, and catch a train to the second. How long it would be before she reached the first of them, with its extraordinary name, she had no idea, and she did not know she had arrived there until the guard pushed her out, suitcases, rug and all, on to the platform.

No one took any notice of her. Darkness fell quickly and she was sure she would freeze to death. It was so cold that she could hardly move by the time the pale dawn came across the sky, but she made her way to the government offices outside the station. The big, bearded men stared at her in amazement, roared with laughter at each other's jokes but made no move to help her. She opened her Bible, showed them her passport and her tickets.

They shrugged their shoulders. "English, no!" shouted one man as he turned away.

Suddenly Gladys had an idea. She thrust her hand inside her coat and pulled out a photograph of her brother, a soldier dressed in all the finery of a drummer-boy in the British army. It did what nothing else could do. They crowded round, chattering and shouting, called to the police and the station-master, and pushed her towards the platform where a train was approaching. Still clutching the photograph, Gladys was heaved aboard and her suitcases thrown after her.

She laughed cheerfully to herself. "They must think I'm a general's sister," she murmured, and settled back on to the hard, uncomfortable seat. Where the train was going she had no idea.

"Vladivostock" said the sign-boards when the train finally reached its destination. From the masts of the ships in the distance she could tell that it was a sea-port. Her eyes brightened at the sight and she almost felt like shouting aloud. Instead, she said a prayer of thanks. She might not be in China but, if she had reached the sea, then she must certainly have travelled right across the whole continent of Asia. Somewhere, far down the coast perhaps, was the coastland of China itself.

* * *

But, as she found out, it was still a very long way off and, later that day, she wondered if she was going to reach it after all.

At the hotel to which she was directed, a dirty building with no paint on the walls and filth on the floors, a man stepped forward—a thin, ugly, suspicious-looking creature. He demanded her passport and put it in his pocket. Next day he came to her room, the passport in his hand. He pointed to the word "missionary".

"Why do you want to go to China?" he asked. "We have a lot of machinery in Russia. You stay here. We need young people to work machines."

"It's not machinery," replied Gladys. "I'm a missionary!" As she spoke she wondered if she would ever stay alive long enough to be one, after all.

The man from the secret police did not understand. "Yes," he said. "You—machinery. You stay in Russia and work machinery!"

It was no use arguing. Terrified that she would be arrested and kept in Russia to work in a factory she slammed the door and locked herself into her room. Not until the next day did the secret policeman come to the door and fling the passport on to the dirty floor. Even then, Gladys had no idea what was going to happen to her. She was so frightened that she hardly dared to leave her room to get something to eat, and she jumped with fright when someone whispered to her as she went through the entrance of the hotel.

"I will come for you to-night. After it's dark I'll knock on your door." As she turned sharply the voice went on. "Don't look round. Pretend I haven't spoken to you. I want to help you." The voice stopped and a girl passed her.

What it was all about Gladys had no idea. Nor did she ever find out who the girl was or how she came to speak English. Later that night, however, there was a tap on her door. Opening it, she saw the girl standing outside.

"Come quickly!"

They sped down the rickety stairs of the hotel, out of the door past the sleeping night-porter, and into the cold, dark streets of the town. There were no lights, except here and there in the windows of a house or an office, and Gladys stumbled again and again as she followed her guide through the alleyways and lanes. At last the ground changed. There were cobbles under her feet. She stumbled over railway-lines and was hauled up by the girl's unexpectedly strong arm. The air grew fresher, and colder. Chains rattled and she heard the splash of water and waves. Stopping at last she saw she was amongst the docks.

The girl pointed to the dark shape of a ship moored nearby. "It is a Japanese ship, and it will sail at dawn. The captain understands. As long as you show him that you are British he will not ask questions."

Gladys hardly knew how to thank her. Clearly she would be in danger for helping her to escape. All she could do was to take the girl's cold hand and squeeze it gratefully. "I have no money," she said, awkwardly.

"It doesn't matter. I'm glad to help you. I wouldn't like to think of you in a prison-camp." Then the girl paused and said hesitantly. "You have no spare clothes? They are very scarce here."

Gladys remembered how she had run out of the hotel in the darkness, leaving suitcases, clothes and the kettle and stove behind. She had not even brought clothes for herself. All she possessed was what she was wearing. "They're in my room at the hotel. Perhaps you could go and get them for yourself?"

"I wouldn't dare. They would know it was I who had helped you and I'd be arrested. Then *I* would be in a prison-camp instead of you."

"I've got those." Gladys found the only things she had brought out of the hotel—a pair of stockings she had stuffed into her pocket. She pulled off her woollen gloves. "You'd better have these, too." The girl took them as if they had been really valuable and put them in her bag. She pointed to a little hut by the water's edge.

"You'll probably find the captain of the ship in there." The next moment she had turned away and Gladys heard her running across the cobbled stones of the docks. In less than a minute she was swallowed up by the darkness.

* * *

Now that she was completely on her own Gladys wondered what to do. It was far too dark to try and find her way back to the hotel if she could not get on the boat—and yet, since she had no money, it did not seem likely that any ship-owner would give her a passage for nothing. She stumbled towards the water's edge and noticed a

21

thin line of light under the door of the small hut. Pushing open the door she saw the room was empty except for a Japanese seaman sitting at a table, with some papers in front of him. He wore a dark blue uniform with golden rings round his sleeves.

"Yes?" he asked.

"I want to get to Japan."

"You have the money for the fare?"

Gladys shook her head. "Nothing at all. No money. No valuables. I'm running away. If I stay here I think they will put me in prison."

The officer seemed to take her word. "You are British?" When Gladys nodded he asked if she had a passport. She thought how fortunate she was to have got it back again in the hotel, and pulled it out of her bag.

The officer took it and flicked it open. "A missionary, and a British citizen, eh? We must help you." He rose from the rickety chair. "Come with me." He motioned her out of the door and led her up the steep, narrow gangway leading to the ship's deck. "It doesn't matter about the money. I will see that you get safely to Japan."

Three days later Gladys arrived in Japan. The British official at the docks did not seem to know what to do with her but bought her a ticket to Kobe where, he said, she was sure to find some missionaries to help her. He seemed very glad to be rid of her when he put her on the train, and she never even had a chance to say more than a brief "Thank you" to the kindly young ship's captain. In the years that followed she was to be treated badly and harshly by a great many Japanese, but she never forgot that it was a Japanese seaman who had saved her life within a month of her leaving the safety of England.

In Kobe, as the British official had promised, there were missionaries who gave her food and a bed. Even better, they provided her with a bath. To Gladys it seemed not weeks but years since she had properly bathed in England or talked in her own language to her own people. She did not know then that, in the future, for many months at a time she would be living in dirt and poverty, never speaking her own language for so long that she would almost forget what it sounded like.

3

THE MOUNTAIN INN

"IT'S no use travelling in clothes like that!"

Gladys looked down at her soiled red dress and dusty coat. "They're the best I've got. In fact, they're *all* I've got."

The missionary, Mrs. Smith, looked at her and laughed. "My dear Gladys, I don't mean they're not good enough to wear when you meet Mrs. Lawson! They're far *too* good. Anyone seeing you on the road in those will think you're a wealthy woman and try to rob you."

"They wouldn't get much. Six shillings is precisely all the money I've got in the world, now."

"Never mind. Out of that beautiful red dress you get, and into these." She held out a pair of wide blue trousers and a blue tunic. Gladys giggled as she looked at them. "I shall look pretty daft in those, shan't I?" The missionary smiled too and then became serious. "You'll probably wear them for the rest of your time in China if you're not in the big towns. You've got to speak Chinese, look Chinese and think Chinese if you're ever going to get near these people and help them. Up in the mountains, where you're going, most of the people have never even seen a European. Your pink skin will frighten them without your wearing what they would think are extraordinary clothes." She handed the blue "suit" over and bustled her

24

out of the room. "In a few minutes you'll be off. Two days travelling up the rough tracks into the mountains, riding on a mule, and you won't worry what you're wearing. You'll only be waiting for the journey to come to an end. Now—hurry up, and let's see if you can pass for a Chinese woman!"

As she donned the Chinese dress Gladys felt that at last she was really in China. The missionaries in Kobe had looked after her for a few days, given her a new feeling of safety after the dangerous journey, and set her on her way by ship and train from Japan to the inland Chinese city of Tientsin. There, for a day or two, she had stayed with a missionary, Mrs. Smith, before setting out on the last lap of the journey to join her pioneer friend, Jeannie Lawson.

"You'll not find her easy to live with," warned Mrs. Smith. "She's determined; when she gets ideas, however wild they are, she just carries them out; but she's a great woman, Gladys. She must be, to live in such a wild place as Yangcheng."

* * *

It was two days later that Gladys saw her new home. Perched on a crag amongst the mountains, surrounded by thick walls and high towers to guard it from enemies and bandits, Yangcheng looked, from a distance, like a fairy-tale town. For thousands of years it had stood there, guarding the long trade-road between east and west, giving shelter to the mule-trains which sought safety there each night. It was no more than a stopping-place but, because travellers needed inns, food and a resting-place for the carriers and the mules, it had grown into a busy town. Its mandarin, or mayor, was an important man and its narrow lanes and broad market-place were crowded. As Gladys rode through the East Gate she had her first glimpse of the place and people she would be living with. Dirty, ramshackle houses; tumbledown inns; a few gaily-dressed women amongst the drab, chattering throngs of peasants; priests in yellow robes; priests in scarlet robes; and, wherever she looked, mules and children.

Outside a tumbledown house her muleteer stopped and shouted. A little woman with white hair, dressed in a blue robe and trousers, came to the door as Gladys slid from the mule. Gladys was not sure what she expected—a smile and a welcome, certainly. Instead the woman stared at her.

"Oh! And who are you?"

"I'm Gladys Aylward."

"Then you'd better come in." Mrs. Lawson stepped inside the dark room. "Are you hungry?" As Gladys followed her inside Mrs. Lawson shouted towards another door and immediately an old, toothless man shambled in. Mrs. Lawson spoke rapidly to him and he bowed to Gladys and smiled widely before he shuffled out of the room.

"That's Yang, the cook," explained Jeannie Lawson. "Now, tell me about yourself while you eat. Then you can go and get your baggage. There doesn't look much of you," she commented, acidly. "I hope you're tough!"

Just how tough she would have to be not even Gladys could have guessed at that moment. All she could think was that she was nearly four hundred miles up-country in China, five thousand miles from her mother's and father's little house in London, and that she might very well never see them again.

The meal of dough-balls and vegetables over, she went out to get her baggage from the mule-train. Half an hour later she came back, on the verge of tears. Her blue clothes were spattered with filth and mud and she was panting for breath.

"The children screamed at me, Jeannie, and some of the women threw mud and dirt at me. They kept on shouting. It sounded like this." She made an attempt at the Chinese words.

" 'Foreign devil', that means. Yes, they hate us and they're afraid of us. They're sure *I'm* a devil because of my white hair. What else can you expect, anyway? They'd never seen a European before I came—and I've only been here a week or two myself. It's a good thing we've got old Yang to reassure them. If they see that we haven't eaten *him* I hope, in time, they'll begin to realize we shan't do *them* any harm, either."

* * *

Slowly the days and weeks passed. Bit by bit Gladys got used to the thought of never seeing any but Chinese faces, never hearing English spoken. With old Yang's help she learned the names of common things about the house and the town. Slowly the attitude of the townspeople began to change. The fear died out of their faces and Gladys and Jeannie Lawson could shoulder their way through the narrow lanes without being abused.

"But we don't seem to be doing much missionary work," commented Gladys. "I can't preach—it's difficult enough to ask for rice or flour in the shops and make them understand. And they don't listen when you talk to them, either." Jeannie herself did not seem to be listening. "Besides, what's the good of staying here? Most of the men are only passing through. They bring the mules into an inn, stay for a night or two nights, and then go on again." She paused, irritated because Jeannie seemed to be thinking of something else. "If only we could make them sit down and listen while you talk to them!"

Jeannie rounded on her, her face alight with excitement. "That's it, Gladys! You've got it! You've hit on the very thing!"

"Whatever do you mean?"

"Why—keep them in one place while we talk to them, of course. We'll open an inn!"

Gladys stared at her in amazement and horror. "An *inn*? Us?"

"Why not? We could charge less than the other inn-keepers. We'd have to do that, anyway, to make them risk staying with foreign devils. We can give them good food and plenty of it. We shan't make much profit, of course, but that doesn't matter. And then, when we've told the muleteers our stories, *they* will go out and tell the stories to everyone else they meet on the road. They may not get them right, of course, but it's a beginning. Splendid, Gladys!" Leaving Gladys staring after her, she ran into the kitchen calling for Yang, explaining excitedly what was in her mind.

Later, they planned the scheme more carefully, working out how many men they could accommodate, how much rice and dough they would need.

"It must have a name, of course," said Gladys.

"I've thought of one. *The Inn of Eight Happinesses.* Don't ask me what they are—but it sounds good."

* * *

A few days later the inn was open. The smell of good cooking floated out into the lane from Yang's kitchen. A newly painted sign stood over the entrance to the court-yard. But, though it was open, no muleteers came in.

"You'll have to stand outside and invite them," ordered Jeannie. "My white hair would scare them off, and Yang is busy in the kitchen. Now, learn these words. *Muyo beatcha . . . muyo goodso . . . how, how, how . . . lai, lai, lai.*"

"What do they mean?"

"We have no bugs; we have no fleas; good, good, good; come, come, come! Now go outside and shout."

But that did not work, either. Perhaps Gladys's Chinese was not good enough or perhaps the sight of her fright-ened the men and the mules. No one turned into the inn.

"Then we shall have to *drag* them in!" decided Jeannie. "Just wait until the first mule in the train comes level with the gate, jump out, grab his harness and pull him into the courtyard. The others will follow easily enough."

"And who's going to do that?" demanded Gladys, mutinously.

Jeannie glared at her. "You are, of course! I'm much too old! If you're not prepared to help run the inn and get it going you may as well go home!"

Gladys was having a taste of Jeannie's stubbornness. She felt that the old woman meant exactly what she said— and home was five thousand miles away across the whole of Asia. She left the room, stood in front of the inn, waited till the first mule appeared, leapt for its bridle like a tiger and dragged it into the courtyard. The man on its back could not help coming with it, for its reins were tied round his arm. He screamed in terror, yelled a long string of abuse at her, pulled himself free of the reins and fled through the gate, joining his comrades who were already tearing down the crowded lane.

"And what do we do now?" Gladys, too, was frightened and angry. "All we've got are half-a-dozen mules and no men!"

"You don't think the men are going to leave the mules here without coming to fetch them, do you? And you certainly won't shift the animals till they've eaten and rested. We'll send Yang to bring the men." She turned to the old man. "Go and find them. Tell them we have good food, cheap lodging, clean floors—and stories. That should fetch them!"

To Gladys's astonishment Yang's announcement produced results. One by one, trembling with fear, the hillmen edged into the yard and then into the inn. Sitting down to big bowls of food they muttered appreciatively to each other. The food *was* good, and there was plenty of it.

"When do we hear the stories?" asked the leader.

Jeannie squatted on the floor and began to talk. All Chinese love stories, and this was a new one altogether—the story of a man called Jesus, who could heal the sick. The muleteers settled back, listening. They asked questions, and then demanded still more stories. When they left in the morning they looked well-fed, well-rested and satisfied. With typical Chinese ceremony, they bowed politely to the two "foreign devils". "It is good," they said, "very good! Everything is good—especially the stories."

"Then send us more people," suggested Jeannie.

The men bowed again. "Yes, certainly. We will tell our friends about it. Everywhere along the mule-trains men will hear and talk of the Inn of Eight Happinesses."

The inn was really open at last.

★　★　★

For weeks and months Gladys and Jeannie worked together, both of them courageous, independent and sometimes stubborn in their various ideas. Gladys, with no chance to speak anything but Chinese if she was going to live in Yangcheng, found the language difficult but not quite as hard as she had feared. If you *had* to talk Chinese, you talked it. It was as simple as that. The inn was always full. The stories passed from man to man and from village to village. Even if the two women were not welcomed in the town and the market-place, at least the early hostility had died away. But, deep down, Gladys was worried. Jeannie Lawson was very old and very tired. Often she looked ill. There were times when Gladys wondered whatever would become of herself if anything happened to the old Scotswoman. Would she be able to stay there on her own? She was soon to find out.

Jeannie, one day, had a fall when Gladys was away. The balcony on which she was standing broke under her slight weight and Jeannie crashed into the courtyard. Though she recovered long enough to see Gladys and talk to her from her bed it was clear that she would never properly get better. She was too old, and too weak after years of hardship in the Chinese hills. At last, there amongst her beloved Chinese people, Jeannie Lawson died.

Gladys Aylward was alone, the only British woman for scores of miles, in the very heart of China.

4

CONVICTS IN REVOLT

"YOU must go and see the Mandarin!"

Yang stood, shuffling his feet, but there was an insistent note in his voice. He seemed astonished that Gladys should refuse such a proper request. The Mandarin was mayor, judge and ruler in Yangcheng. He could send men to prison, have them beheaded or turn them out of the town as he pleased. He could, as Yang pointed out, close down the Inn of the Eight Happinesses if he chose to do so, or have Gladys arrested for not showing him proper respect. And now, since the inn was really a missionary station, that would be a terrible thing.

"But I've never seen him, and I wouldn't know what to say."

Yang shuffled again. "You would bow, and . . . and . . ." Yang paused, uncertain of just what she *should* say. After all he was only a poor cook. He had never spoken to a mandarin in his life. "I will go and find out what you should say. But now that Mrs. Lawson is dead and you are the head of the mission you should certainly go and pay him your respects."

A day or so later, since he had not mentioned the subject again, Gladys brought it up herself.

"What am I to say to the Mandarin, Yang?"

Gladys thought he looked amused. "I have asked in the *yamen* (the Mandarin's home and court-house). He does not receive women. So you need not go." Yang turned away to the kitchen without another word, and Gladys sighed with relief.

* * *

It was all the more astonishing, therefore, when Yang rushed into the inn a little while later. He could hardly speak for excitement and, when he did, Gladys could hardly credit his news.

"The Mandarin is coming."

"Where?"

"Here. To the inn. He's in the street now."

"But why?" Gladys felt a twinge of uneasiness. Perhaps she ought to have gone and paid her respects to him, after all.

"He wants to see you."

She had no time to ask more, for already there was a commotion in the courtyard. Wiping her hands down her faded blue robe she stood on the veranda, staring at the colourful spectacle. There were servants everywhere. In the gateway a chattering, curious crowd had already gathered and were trying to push their way in. Scholars and priests stood silently by a sedan chair, which had just been set down in the centre of the courtyard by four carriers. The curtains covering the chair were gently moved aside and out stepped an elderly man in a scarlet robe, wearing a black cap. To Gladys, he seemed so gentle and so dignified that she hardly felt he could have come to arrest her, after all.

34

After they had exchanged the usual long, formal Chinese greetings the Mandarin explained why he had come.

For many centuries it had been the custom in China to bind the feet of tiny baby girls, curling their toes beneath the soles. The smaller the feet, it had been thought, the greater a woman's dignity. True, they could not walk far or easily, but that did not matter. It was the custom of the country. Now the Government had issued a law that no women's feet should be bound any longer, and those who had such feet should have them loosed. Every mandarin was ordered to find someone who would make sure that this was done.

"I want you to find me someone to do this. Your Christian missions must be able to send a woman to me. She will be paid, of course. A little grain and about a farthing for every woman she attends to. It will mean going out into the villages for many miles around, all through the hills. Because that is dangerous she will be given soldiers to protect her. That is all!"

They bowed to each other. Then the Mandarin climbed into his chair and was borne away, leaving Gladys to wonder whatever she was going to do.

She was no nearer to a solution when the Mandarin came for an answer, several weeks later. None of the missions could spare a woman missionary to go round inspecting feet, though she hardly dared put it in quite that way to the Mandarin. All she could do was explain that she had made many inquiries but could find no one to help. The Mandarin did not seem surprised.

"Then you must do it yourself!"Before she had time to

35

protest he went on. "I appoint you my official Inspector of Women's Feet!"

Gladys could have howled with laughter. She had come five thousand miles to China to be a missionary, and then this happened! Suddenly she had an idea. "You wouldn't have any objection if I told these women the Christian stories I tell in the inn?"

"You can preach what you like, and convert whom you like—as long as you do what I order. Make sure that the feet of every woman under my rule are unbound!"

* * *

The months that followed proved to Gladys that God Himself had sent the Mandarin to her. In Yangcheng she would have been able to preach to the muleteers who stayed for a night at the inn and to those few of the towns-people who would listen. No more than that. Now, with soldiers to guarantee her safety and protect her from the brigands that infested the mountain tracks, she was able to visit not merely a dozen or a score of villages in the immediate neighbourhood of Yangcheng, but to find her way to hundreds of villages and hamlets in the area. The Mandarin's order, which she carried written on official red paper, made her task easier than it might have been, and the presence of the soldiers proved her authority. But to Gladys herself, though she was glad to see an end of the horrible practice of foot-binding and was happy to give new freedom to tiny children before their feet had been ruined for life, the really important thing was that, everywhere she went, she was able to tell these simple village people the Gospel story. Seldom did she come across anyone who had ever heard of Jesus. Almost everybody was afraid of evil spirits. It was a joy to tell them of Jesus, who would cast out their fears and change their lives.

In a few months, instead of being known as the strange missionary woman in Yangcheng who ran an inn, Gladys was widely known through the whole countryside. Her Chinese swiftly improved, and her knowledge of the many hill-dialects grew with it. Very few people could understand how far England was from Yangcheng or how much courage it had taken for her to make so long a journey. To them, the treks into the hills were still more dangerous, and even the Mandarin complimented her on her courage.

She was to need all the courage she could summon up before many months had passed—and the result of her next terrifying experience was to give her a completely new reputation.

*　*　*

One day a messenger dashed into the courtyard of the inn, waving a red paper in his hand. He thrust it at her and she read it to old Yang.

"It's a message from the Mandarin. There's a riot in the prison. But I can't understand why *I* should be told."

"You'll have to go if the message comes from the *yamen*."

"Rubbish!" replied Gladys. "A riot has nothing to do with me." She turned to the messenger. "Go back to the *yamen* and tell the Mandarin I have a lot of people at the inn, and I'm busy."

The startled servant bowed and ran out. It was not long, however, before he was back again, waving the message on the red paper more urgently than ever. Exasperated, Gladys wiped her hands, pulled her drab gown into place and set off after him. He led her, not to the *yamen*, but to the prison, and long before she reached it she could hear the uproar going on inside. There were constant shrieks of terror and pain, and the prison governor stood at the entrance, wringing his hands.

"The prisoners have rioted!"

"So I can hear," answered Gladys sharply. "Why?"

"I don't know. Nobody ever knows why these things happen. The convicts were in the yard and one of them went mad." He led her to the entrance and she looked through the bars of the thick gate. "Look! There he is— the big man with a chopper. He found it in the yard and went mad and he's attacking everyone with it. He's killed one or two men already and the others are fighting each other, too."

"Why don't you stop them?"

The governor was shaking with fear. "They'd kill me if I went inside. That's why I've sent for *you*. Nobody but *you* would dare to go inside!"

Gladys wondered if she had properly heard him. "Me?" she demanded. "Go in there? I wouldn't dream of it."

The governor looked at her in astonishment. "But you say you have the spirit of the Living God within you. You are a Christian. Your God will not let anything happen to *you*!"

After that there did not seem to be anything else to do

but turn the key, open the gate and step into the gruesome courtyard, where wounded men lay on the ground all round her. Slowly the shouts and screams died away as the convicts saw her. Then, at the other side of the yard, she saw the madman. His eyes seemed to blaze. In his hands he held a huge axe. Suddenly he let out a high-pitched scream of fury and rushed towards her, the axe held high in the air. Gladys stood completely still, too frightened even to turn and run for the gate. A couple of paces from her the murderer stopped, glaring at her.

"Give me that axe!" None of her fear showed in her voice.

Slowly the madness died out of the man's eyes. He stepped forward, wiped the blood off the handle and laid the axe in her hands. Before she went forward to speak to the man she passed the weapon through the gate to the governor. Then, for an hour, as the wounded men were carried away, she talked to the convicts. She saw the tiny wooden cages round the courtyard in which they were kept, heard their stories as she spoke to a murderer, a thief, a priest who had turned robber, and many others. Many of them had been there for years, most of them would never be released. She thought to herself that she, too, would go mad if she were as bored as they were. Then, as the men quietly went back to the cages and were locked in, she marched out to talk to the governor.

"You're turning them into animals," she said. "They have nothing to do all day and a riot is just one way of getting some excitement."

"Of course they have nothing to do. What *can* they do? They're criminals."

"I will talk to the Mandarin." She spoke as if he were an old friend, instead of the ruler of the whole district. Indeed, in the months she had been visiting the villages and reporting back to him, he *had* become a friend. In the court, the *yamen*, where no women were expected to come, she spoke to him as if she were his equal, and for his part the Mandarin found himself asking her advice about conditions in the villages and even in the city itself. Yet her promise to get the conditions of the prisoners changed was not as easy to fulfil as she had hoped.

"All prisons in China are like that," replied the Mandarin. "We have no money to give them better conditions —and if we did make life easier they would only take advantage of it. Why should we bother to help men who are thieves and murderers?"

"Perhaps if they were able to earn money honestly they wouldn't want to be thieves and murderers."

The Mandarin shrugged his thin shoulders. "Do what you like. You have some strange ideas, but they very often seem to work out right." As she bowed and turned away he tapped his stick and brought her back. "The governor of the prison is very grateful for what you did. He says you can go to the prison whenever you like and talk to the convicts."

* * *

Gladys smiled happily. In a strange way she had found another congregation to preach to. First the muleteers in the inn, then the village women as she unbound the children's feet, and now a congregation that could not run away, a group of wild men in prison. It was not long

40

before two looms were installed in the prison—Gladys managed to get them from friends of the governor—and some cotton yarn for the men to start weaving. Then she found a miller's wheel. The men sold the cloth they wove and the corn they ground. With a little money of their own they began to feel independent and hopeful once more. In time some of them would be able to pay the debts they owed and go free. Then she got hold of some rabbits for the prisoners to breed and sell. Almost every day, when she was not acting as a Foot Inspector in the villages, she visited the prison, talked to the convicts about health and hygiene and told them stories from the New Testament. The prison governor, like the Mandarin, became her friend. But, even so, she was surprised one day when he told her he had a request to make.

"I have a friend coming to Yangcheng to stay with me. He is a great scholar but he is a Christian, too. I would like him to preach in your mission at the inn."

If Gladys was surprised by the request the governor was even more astonished at her reply.

"Thank you. I would like him to do that. But I am going to make one condition. I would like him to preach to the convicts, too."

"Here in the prison? Yes, he can do that."

"No. Not here. I want them to come to the inn, and he can preach to them in my church."

The governor was horrified. "They would all escape!"

"With those big chains on? Nonsense. They wouldn't stand a chance. And, anyway, I will tell them they mustn't try to run away. They will do what I say!"

The governor did not even argue. The Mandarin was sure to agree with the foreign woman. Anyway, she was probably right. She usually was right. And if she told the convicts to behave he had no doubt they would do so. A week later, to the astonishment of the inhabitants of Yangcheng, who came running from all directions to see the strange sight, the convicts marched through the crowded streets to the Inn of Eight Happinesses, and went to church.

★ ★ ★

One of Gladys's strangest experiences happened in a prison, just like the one in Yangcheng. She had found that, in a city where she was staying, few Christians visited the prison and certainly nobody preached there. She gained the governor's permission and visited it each day, teaching the convicts to sing Christian choruses and telling them the stories of Jesus.

Amongst the prisoners was a young man who had committed murder. For some reason he had not been executed but had been sent to prison instead. Amongst the prisoners he had a great reputation as a mimic, and he was never more popular than when he was mimicking Gladys herself. He would stand on a stool, after she was gone, pull his face into an imitation of hers and, using the same gestures and tones of voice, send his fellow-prisoners into howls of laughter. Then, one day, he found he could not go on. He could not say the things the missionary had said. Trying once more, he stuck at the same point. Suddenly one of the other convicts pulled him down off the stool.

"You know why you can't say what she says, don't you? Because you don't believe it, and she does. You're doing a bad thing, making fun of someone who teaches us about God."

The young convict shrugged his shoulders and wandered away. Some time later, however, he became involved in a fight with another prisoner and was only dragged off him after a struggle, by the prison warders. Brought before the governor he was condemned to the cells, instead of being able to walk freely in the prison courtyard, and was heavily chained at the wrists and ankles. He was like this when Gladys herself went to visit him. Instead of telling him he should not have made fun of her—for she thought his imitation was really very good—she prayed that God would speak to him and free his mind from the chains that bound his soul.

Two days afterwards she visited the prison once more and the young man asked for her at once. His hands and ankles were free.

"What happened to your chains?" she asked.

He looked at her with a strange expression. "They fell off," he replied simply.

"What do you mean?"

"I don't know how it happened," he went on. "Nor do any of the men who were sleeping in my cell. But last night I wakened up, like Peter in the prison in Jerusalem, and I was sure Jesus Himself was in the cell with me. I couldn't see Him, but I called the others to tell them He was there. Then, suddenly, He was gone. But my chains . . ." he paused, as if he were still not sure it could be true. "My chains," he said at last, "had fallen off. They

43

were on the floor by my side. You can ask any of the convicts who were in the cell—or the warders who came in when they heard us moving. It's true. And Jesus has freed me from my sins, too. I want to be a Christian."

5

"NINEPENCE"

GLADYS had been in Yangcheng for two years when her first child arrived. It was a small girl, and she bought her for ninepence.

Month by month she went out into the villages, carrying out the Mandarin's orders, seeing the women's and girls' feet were unbound, and that those which had had the bandages removed were not wrapped up again. Wherever she went, she preached. Very few of those who listened understood everything she talked about, but they learned to love Jesus. Because of that, their lives were changed. Husbands treated their wives more kindly. Boys had always been welcome in Chinese homes but girl-babies had been regarded as a nuisance. In Christian homes, however, even girl-babies were properly cared for.

At the Inn of the Eight Happinesses a good deal of building work had been done and it now contained a small chapel. Not only in the hill-villages but in Yangcheng itself there were those who were converted to the Christian way and who met, week by week, for worship, prayer and Bible study. One of the staunchest of the little Christian group was Hsi-lien, the first muleteer whom she had dragged into the compound of the inn the first night it opened. Yang remained with her, but now he was not only the cook but a splendid helper who was even better

at telling stories than Gladys herself—even if he did sometimes get Moses, Jonah and the Good Samaritan rather
mixed up with each other! The Mandarin, too, was be-
coming a close friend.

But, two years after she had taken on the office of Foot
Inspector, she had her first real clash with him.

*   *   *

She had been to a village called Chowtsun and was on
her way back through the Yangcheng streets to report
to him when she noticed a woman sitting by the side of
the road. She was obviously a tribal woman from the
hills. Her brightly-coloured clothes, now faded with the
sun, her great silver earrings and necklace, and the green
puttees she wore round the bottom of her baggy trousers,
showed that she did not belong to Yangcheng. As Gladys
looked at her she thought she had seldom seen anyone
with a more wicked or cruel face. Then she looked down
and saw the child in the woman's lap. It was as thin as if
it had lived through a famine, and its eyes were deep-sunk
and terrified.

"That child is ill," snapped Gladys. "She needs
medicine."

"Bah!" retorted the woman, "she's all right. I'll sell her
to you for two dollars!"

Gladys was horrified. "I don't want her. Look after her
yourself, and do it properly!"

"You can have her for a dollar and a half, then."

"You're a very wicked woman. I haven't got a dollar
and a half"—which was quite true—"and I can't see why
any mother should want to sell her child."

46

The evil look deepened on the cruel face, and suddenly Gladys realized the truth. The woman was not the child's mother at all. She had stolen the baby from some village and was trying to sell her in the town to anyone who might want a child. Saying no more, she hurried on to the *yamen*, the Mandarin's residence. When she had made her report about her visit to Chowtsun she asked a question.

"What do you do with women who steal children?"

The Mandarin raised his eyebrows in surprise. "Nothing."

"Why not? You make the laws here in Yangcheng and they're supposed to be good laws. Women like that should be put in prison. And there's one of them in the town now. She tried to sell me the child!"

The Mandarin smiled smoothly. "I shouldn't buy it. You have enough to do without looking after a child."

"I have no intention of buying it. But you *must* do something!"

"These women do not work alone. They belong to gangs of robbers and raiders from the hills. If I put her in prison, or did anything to punish her, the robbers would raid the town, or burn some of the houses. Anyway, why should I bother about a baby girl? I suppose it *was* a girl? It's usually girls that these women steal, and then they sell them as slaves." He turned and banged his gong sharply and angrily. The audience was at an end. "I give you an order. You are to do nothing and you are not to speak to the woman!"

Gladys turned to the door, and then swung round, furiously. "I shall take no notice of your order! I came to

China to preach the love of Jesus, not to inspect women's feet. And I shall show these people, and you, just what love really means."

For a moment the Mandarin's hand shook in his scarlet robe as he held his stick, glaring at her as if he were going to clang the gong again and have the missionary-woman arrested. Then a new look passed over his face. He gazed after Gladys with a strange respect. It was the first time, so far as he could remember, that anyone had ever dared to argue with him, to refuse to obey an order. Certainly it was the first time in his life that a *woman* had done so.

Gladys walked down the street, sandals clacking swiftly on the cobbled stones. She had no need to speak to the woman, for the robber herself spoke first.

"I'll give it to you for a dollar!" she whined.

Taking the few coins she possessed from her purse, Gladys shook them into the child-stealer's hand. "This is all I have. About ninepence, I should think."

"Yah! Take it then!" And Gladys found herself holding the filthy little bundle of skin and bones, wrapped round with a few rags.

Back in the inn she put the child on the floor and unwrapped it. The Mandarin was right. It was a girl, so thin that Gladys felt she could hardly live another day. But live she did, though for days and nights she ran away like an animal, hiding in a corner when anyone came near, eating whatever food Yang put down for her and then dashing into hiding again.

But, by the end of a fortnight, "Ninepence" (as she was always to be nicknamed) was clean, tidy, and gay, while the skinny little body had already begun to show signs of health. She was the first of Gladys's family.

*   *   *

The second arrived a few months later.

Ninepence came into the inn one day with a gleam in her eye. "Can I have a bit less for dinner?"

Her "mother" gazed at her in astonishment, for Nine-pence usually ate everything that came her way. But she nodded, warily.

"Would you be ready to have a bit less, too?"

"What's all this about?" demanded Gladys, sus-piciously.

"If you did have a bit less, and I had a bit less, we could put the two 'lesses' in a bowl and there would be enough for another one!"

"Another what?"

"Another little boy, of course," replied Ninepence. "He's outside. He doesn't belong to anybody because I've asked him, and he hasn't had anything to eat for days."

"He must belong to somebody!"

But Ninepence was already running out of the gate, to come back immediately holding a shy, hungry boy by the hand. "This is 'Less'," she announced.

And from that moment—for Gladys never did find his parents—"Less" joined the family in the inn.

The third small boy came to them when they were up the river, washing clothes. One minute there was nobody else there. Then Bao-bao was by their side. Where he came from they never found out, though they searched the valley for someone to whom he might belong. The fourth came with a crowd of refugees who were escaping from floods on the Yellow River—a small boy named Francis—and the fifth was a little girl brought to the Mandarin's court because she was completely lost, and handed over by him to the best person he could find to look after her.

*　　*　　*

So Gladys's family grew, bit by bit, and the Mandarin became her close friend. She had not spoken English for years, except on odd occasions when she went from the hills to one of the mission stations, and she spoke the many hill-dialects as naturally as the Chinese themselves. Far away in the hills, the people of Yangcheng were more concerned about the crops, the cattle and the price of grain than they were about what was happening in the great world beyond the river and the plains. They noticed the things that happened to themselves and their own countryside, and very little else. There were bitterly cold winters they would always remember . . . floods on the great Yellow River . . . refugees who filled the town. If anyone had told them that the Japanese, who were fighting in other parts of China, had invaded their own province of Shansi they would have merely shrugged their shoulders. Whoever these Japanese were they would not come to Yangcheng.

Then, one day in the spring of 1938, a group of small, silvery aeroplanes came flying in over the mountains.

There were few people in Yangcheng who had ever seen an aeroplane, and from every house and building men, women and children came dashing out, crowding together in the narrow streets and lanes to stare upwards as the planes swept nearer. They flew round the town, turned away towards the mountains, circled back and then dipped towards Yangcheng, bearing down on it in a swift-moving, silver line. Only when it was too late to do anything did the townspeople understand their danger. From the planes, as they roared down towards the thronged streets and zoomed upwards again, came stick after stick of bombs, raining down on the old town, and exploding in the streets. There was no time to try and escape, and even if they had been in the houses there would have been little hope for many of the victims, for houses, shops and temples were blitzed all over the town.

Yangcheng had had its first taste of war, and in the bombing scores of innocent people were killed. The Japanese invasion of China had reached Shansi and its mountain strongholds.

Gladys Aylward was not in the streets to see the aircraft. She was busy at the Inn of Eight Happinesses. The first she knew of what was happening was when she heard the first explosions in the streets and the screams that followed them. The next thing she knew was that the floor on which she stood was collapsing and the house was crashing down above her.

6

THE MANDARIN'S FEAST

"I THINK she's alive."

Gladys tried to move. "Of course I'm alive," she tried to shout. But her mouth was full of dust and dirt. The floor and part of the roof was piled on top of her, and she could neither move nor make herself heard. Above her she could hear Yang's voice and the excited shouts of men whom he had called in to help him. There came the sound of stones being shifted. The old timbers creaked as they were dragged away and she only hoped that, as the men tried to extricate her, they would not release another avalanche of stones on top of her. Bit by bit the rubble was cleared away and she was dragged out, bruised, cut here and there, and completely filthy, but still very much alive.

"Never say die!" she said, spitting out the dust and dirt. "It was the Japanese, of course?"

Yang nodded miserably. There were tears running down the dirt on his face. "Lots of the houses are smashed, and dozens of people have been killed by the bombs."

Gladys steadied herself for a minute or two and then went out from the rubbish-filled courtyard to see for herself what had happened. She was too horrified even to weep. Everywhere there were wounded people, and it was clear that many, as Yang had said, had been killed in the surprise attack. She had heard a good deal about the way in which the Japanese attacked undefended towns, but it was hard to believe that the innocent people of Yangcheng, an ordinary hill-town which was little more than a staging-post for mule-teams, should have suffered in this way. She shook the dust from her tattered gown, wiped the blood from her face and set out to organize the relief work that must be undertaken.

*   *   *

As she talked to the Mandarin and the prison governor she found they had the same ideas. It was clear that the bombing was only the beginning. It showed that the Japanese army was not far away, and would probably soon try to capture the city as they marched forward. There were no soldiers in Yangcheng, but there were plenty of armed Chinese in the hills round about and in the villages of the plains and they would come in and try to defend the city. There would be a battle, and probably the city would be destroyed.

"We must leave Yangcheng," said the Mandarin sadly. "And everyone who is able to move must come with us."

Gladys nodded. "But first we must do what we can to help the wounded. Are there any places we can use as dressing-stations to patch up their wounds?"

"Only two temples have been unharmed. But we can use those."

"My convicts are clearing the roads of rubbish. They can carry the wounded to the temples," put in the prison governor.

"Good." Gladys nodded as cheerfully as she could. "I

haven't much first-aid stuff,but there is a little in the inn if it hasn't all been smashed to bits. And we can use cotton cloth to make bandages. Come on. Let's get to work." She turned to the Mandarin. "You must arrange to get the wounded carried out of the town."

He clanged his gong, and gave swift instructions to the servants standing by. "Where will *you* go?" he asked Gladys.

"There is a little village called Bei Chai Chuang away up in the hills, where some people have become Christians. I'll take some of our Christians from Yangcheng up there when the darkness comes. Old Yang will help me." As she was going out she stopped. "When the Japanese have come and gone again we'll return, of course. They never stay long. They're always on the march, looking for another town to conquer and burn." She smiled, suddenly. "But I'm afraid my job as the Mandarin's Inspector of Feet is finished!"

* * *

During the next day or so she seemed to be all over the town, with her first-aid box and a word of encouragement for the wounded, the children, the convicts and the muleteers who were working hard to clear the streets.

Five days after the bombing, when the Japanese soldiers entered the town, the East and West Gates were wide open. But houses, shops, inns and temples were deserted. The whole town was empty and the population of Yangcheng was somewhere out in the hills.

From her hide-out at Bei Chai Chuang, a tiny hamlet of eight houses, Gladys waited for news. When none came she made up her mind to find out for herself what was happening. Making her way down the narrow paths and tracks through the mountains she trudged on till she came in sight of Yangcheng. The sun was dropping towards the distant horizon as she stared thoughtfully towards the walls. She could see no sign of movement at the gates or on the walls themselves. With eyes now long accustomed to the district she watched the countryside below the town—the paddy-field, the grain-fields, the river. Nothing moved anywhere. Slowly she made her way forward, expecting that at any moment a rifle would crack out in the silence and a bullet flatten itself on the rocks by her side. Nothing of the kind happened. As she stepped on to the broader path leading to the town the silence was eerie and frightening, but it seemed that, unless all the Japanese were keeping in hiding to take her by surprise, the enemy had gone.

Her wooden sandals clacked on the cobbled street as she stepped through the West Gate. Here and there a house still smoked where it smouldered, but there was a deathly quietness everywhere. Then, as she passed an empty inn, she almost screamed. From the doorway came the sound of a cackling laugh. Gazing into the shadows she saw a filthy beggar, an old twisted man who went on laughing.

"So you've come back to be killed, eh?" he shrilled at her.

"The Japanese have gone," she replied. "What are you doing here?"

"They won't hurt an old man like me—an old beggar with no money and no sense. But you're wrong. They

55

haven't gone. That was only an advance patrol that came to spy out the town. The real army is on its way."

"How do you know?" Gladys felt he was slightly mad.

"I heard men talking. The others are coming to-day."

Before she could ask any more questions she knew the old beggar was speaking the truth. Not far away, where the East Gate still remained closed, there was an explosion and the sound of smashing timber, followed by shrill voices as the Japanese soldiers began to break into the town once more. Then, all at once, Gladys found the town was not as empty as it had seemed. From the houses at the further side, towards the gate, came the whine of bullets. Chinese soldiers had occupied the town after the Japanese patrols had left and were encamped in hiding-places in the hills above it and round it.

If the Japanese were at the East gate they would soon make their way round to the West Gate by which she had entered. She knew now that she had spent too long trying to explore the seemingly-deserted city. She was trapped.

As she stood, undecided what to do, the sun dipped behind the hills and the quick-falling darkness began to spread over the landscape. It was just possible, after all, that she might manage to escape.

So far the West Gate was unmanned and unattacked. She dodged through it in the twilight and moved to the rocks and bushes by its side. Below her, in the fields, she could see the khaki figures of the little Japanese soldiers moving to and fro—one company to the east of the town, the other to the west. It was hardly a chance, but she knew she must take it. Slipping and sliding as quickly as she dared she made her way down to the fields which lay between the two Japanese companies and flung herself into the fields of grain. Terrified of what would happen if she were caught she crawled and scrambled forward through the corn, with the voices of the Japanese only a few yards away. Then, at last, they grew more distant and she knew she was safe. Rising to her feet in the darkness she began to run, stumbling on and on until she felt beneath her feet the track which led to Bei Chai Chuang.

★   ★   ★

Gladys remained in the mountain village from the summer of 1938 to the spring of 1939, every now and again making occasional visits to other villages and to Yangcheng, which the Japanese had now deserted once more. In a large cave in the hills nearby she fitted up an emergency hospital, caring as well as she could for the injured and the sick. It was desperately cold through the winter months, and food was scarce. The townsfolk were anxious about friends and relatives who had scattered to other villages, and there was always talk of going "back home". Gladys kept in touch with the Mandarin throughout the long winter, hearing news of what the Chinese Government was doing, and of the advance of the Japanese armies all over the great sprawling land of China. At last the Mandarin came to a decision.

"We must go back to Yangcheng—but not for long. I shall send the town-crier out to summon the people from the villages where they have scattered. The Government has said that every town and all our crops are to be destroyed, so that they are no use to the Japanese if they come back."

"You mean we've got to pull everything down?"

The Mandarin nodded sadly. "We will save what we can and take it with us . . . gather what crops we can find . . . set the houses on fire and go away." He suddenly smiled; a secret sort of smile, Gladys thought. "There is something else I want to do, too. I am going to give a feast."

If Gladys thought it was an odd time to have a feast she did not say so. The Mandarin was the most important man in the district. No doubt he wished to say farewell to all those who had helped him—the clerks, the officials, the prison governor and the like. She was astonished when he insisted that she should be there, too. Women did not meet equally with men in the interior of China, nor go to official occasions such as this. But, if he ordered her to do so, she could hardly disobey.

*　　*　　*

The Mandarin's feast was the last great gathering in Yangcheng. For days the men had worked feverishly in the town, saving whatever might be carried away to the villages—furniture, rags, cooking-pots, timber. The women had gathered everything they could from the fields. Building after building was destroyed. Even the temples were pulled down and, when the townspeople were afraid to destroy the Temple of the Great Scorpion in case the legendary creature might escape and devour them, the Christians pulled it down for them, singing hymns as they did so.

Before she went to the half-ruined *yamen* for the feast Gladys paid her last visit to the Inn of the Eight Happinesses. There was no need to destroy *that*. Bombing and the winter weather had made it useless. She stood in the cluttered courtyard, wondering just how much she had achieved in her eight crowded years in Yangcheng. A good many people had become Christians in the town and in the villages round about. The mule-teams had carried the Gospel far away. Even some of the convicts had learned the Gospel. But sometimes it seemed a long time and terribly hard work for very little result. Most of those who had believed the Gospel had been very ordinary people, and the leaders of the town had remained unconvinced, choosing to follow the old ways of their forefathers.

She went on to the feast. The Mandarin's scarlet robes were faded, and the prison governor looked haggard and ill. It was true of all those who sat round the room, too, and Gladys knew that she must look as ill, hungry and tattered as the rest.

When the meal was over and the long ceremonious service of the frugal dishes finished for the last time in Yangcheng, the Mandarin rose to speak. He thanked all those who had stood by him during the year, who had been his friends and associates for many years before the Japanese came and before the missionary ever arrived in Yangcheng. He told of the plans for the future. He paid tribute to Gladys—*Ai-wai-deh*, he called her, "the good woman"—for all she had done since she came to Yangcheng. He talked of her work at the inn, how she stopped the riot at the prison and gave new hope to the convicts, and how she had given freedom to the women of the hills.

"No one else could have done these things," he said, very seriously. "Only a woman in whom lived the Spirit

59

of the Living God." He turned to Gladys. "I have listened to you and argued with you. I have seen the life
you live. And now I know that the Gospel you preach is
true." In his worn, scarlet robes, with all the majesty of a
man who has commanded men all his life, he bowed
to her.

"*Ai-wai-deh*," he said, quietly, "before we leave
Yangcheng, this city that has been my home and yours,
there is one more thing I must do. I want to become a
Christian."

7

WANTED BY THE ENEMY

"I DON'T think I want to buy the murderers," said Gladys, uncertainly.

The prison governor looked sympathetic, but worried. "They'll have to be killed if you don't."

"Anyway, I haven't got enough money."

Gladys was able to laugh at most things, but this situation seemed too ridiculous for words. The governor had posted up a notice on the prison gates, at Gladys's suggestion, saying that any relative who was willing to pay ninety cents could buy the freedom of any of the convicts if he was willing to guarantee their good behaviour. Otherwise they would have to be killed before Yangcheng was evacuated. Most of the prisoners had been set free. Gladys herself had bought the freedom of two men who had become her friends. Now there were only about eight left. Their relatives were in villages too far away to see the notices or hear the message which the town-crier was announcing. Some of them were thieves; others were murderers.

"All right!" Gladys looked unhappily at the men, sitting dejectedly with iron fetters on their wrists. "I'll tell you what I'll do. Let them go free, and I will make sure they go to their homes, and that their relatives pay you the money. I'll collect it from them and pay you if we ever get back to Yangcheng."

Happy to do whatever *Ai-wai-deh* suggested, the governor had the chains struck off the men and they trailed out of the prison after her. Gladys thought to herself that she was collecting a very strange group of people who depended on her. Not only had she Ninepence, Less, and her first children. That little family had grown by dozens until she was caring for about a hundred children, many of them refugees and boys and girls whose parents had been killed in the bombing. Now she had a group of bandits to add to them. And, as she was leaving the prison, an official from the Mandarin's court caught up with her.

"I have a slave-girl in the women's court and I don't know what to do with her. She's called Sualan. She's only about fifteen, and we haven't been able to arrange a marriage for her." He hardly waited for Gladys to ask any questions. "She *can* go with you, of course?"

So Gladys's family grew. The convicts proved no trouble at all, being only too grateful to be out of prison at last, and she was able to restore them to their families, collect the money for them and eventually repay it to the governor. But Sualan, Ninepence, Less and a great many more of the children were to be in her care for a long time to come.

* * *

The months that followed grew more and more frightening and terrible. The Japanese, now fighting all over China, moved swiftly from place to place. Their forces were not big enough to occupy the whole of China, and so they marched here and there, capturing a town, ill-treating the inhabitants who remained within it, murdering the leading citizens and anyone who might raise opposition against them, taking what food they could lay hands on, and, after staying for a week or so, or sometimes only for a few days, moving on elsewhere. The Christians they disliked intensely, partly because they were closely linked with "Western" missions and partly because of their faith and courage.

The Japanese might turn up anywhere at any moment, especially in the towns on the main roads, and when the soldiers were not to be seen aircraft might suddenly appear to bomb the cities and machine-gun the crowds in the streets and on the country roads. It was an awful time to be living in China but, even so, never once did Gladys regret coming. She believed that God had sent her to preach to these people and help them. More than once Japanese Christians serving in the army were found in the services she conducted in one town or another, for she often had to live in towns which the Japanese were occupying for a while. If she was frightened—and there were occasions when she was very frightened indeed—it was not because of her own safety or what might happen to her, but because if she were killed, she could not be certain that anyone would look after the crowd of olive-skinned, ragged, smiling children she had collected.

And yet, as though God were keeping her safe because there was still more work for her to do, she managed to stay alive and free.

That does not mean that she did not suffer. From time to time she fell ill. She was often hungry—more hungry than most people, because she was always ready to give away her own food to the children or the people with whom she happened to be living. Now and again she was ill-treated. Once she was knocked about and beaten up so badly by a group of Japanese soldiers, who thought she was a spy for the Chinese Government, that she did not really get over the experience for months. The Japanese authorities were not far wrong in their suspicions. She *was* helping the Chinese authorities, passing on whatever information came her way about troop-movements and whatever plans she could discover. This she felt she must do, whatever happened, for China was far more her country than Britain. Because she loved its people and wanted really to belong to them, she had become a citizen of China in 1936.

*   *   *

During the nightmare years that followed the evacuation of Yangcheng she moved from one place to another, sometimes taking the children with her, sometimes almost on her own.

For a long time she stayed in the hospital-cave at Bei Chai Chuang, up in the hills. Later she moved down, with a few of her children and friends, to the town of Chin Shui. Here, when the Japanese approached the town, she was led away by two boys, Timothy and Wan Yu, to a little house in the hills belonging to one of their relatives. Safe for a while, she visited the houses in the neighbour- hood, preaching and encouraging the peasants. Then, one day, Timothy came rushing in.

"The soldiers are at the other end of the village!"

There was no time to hide. Timothy, Wan Yu and the

folk in the house waited for the door of the compound to burst open, and Gladys stared through the window at the approaching soldiers, whose rifles had bayonets attached. She saw them go into house after house, finding them empty because the owners had been more quickly warned of their coming.

Hoping to gain time for Wan Yu's family to escape, she went out into the yard and put her hand on the gate. If she swung it open the sight of a "foreign devil" must hold up the soldiers who would spend time questioning her before they killed her. In the confusion the people inside might perhaps be forgotten. Her hands were trembling as she fumbled at the latch and she paused for a moment to pray for courage. In that moment Wan Yu dashed out of the house.

"Stop! Stop, *Ai-wai-deh*! The soldiers have turned back! They're going down the hill!"

Gladys almost collapsed with relief but, once inside the house, called the little group together to thank God for their escape.

*　　*　　*

From Chin Shui she went on to the bigger town of Tsehchow, the headquarters of a mission station, where she stayed with some of her missionary friends. It was while she was there that a message was circulated from Madame Chiang Kai-Shek, the wife of the head of the Chinese Government, and herself a Christian. It said that she had begun a fund to help war orphans, and that a centre had been set up in the town of Sian, far across the great Yellow River, where they would be cared for. To the missionaries in Tsehchow it was wonderful news. There had always been orphans in the school at Tsehchow, but now there were far more than could possibly be fed and housed. Two hundred children were crowded into the buildings.

"We can't send them all, of course," said one of the missionaries. "I should think we ought to try and look after half of them ourselves and send the other hundred to Sian."

This was agreed. One hundred of the children were chosen to undertake the long journey and, to the relief of everyone in Tsehchow, it was learned five weeks later that they had arrived safely.

The incident gave Gladys a good deal to think about. For some time she had been more or less on her own. Ninepence and the rest of the orphans had not gone to Tsehchow but after living for months in the hills had finally gone back to the ruined city of Yangcheng after the Japanese had moved on.

"They really ought to be moved to Sian, with the rest of the orphans," urged the Tsehchow missionaries.

"But who would take them?"

"Why, you, of course."

This was what Gladys had been dreading that they would suggest. She knew that perhaps she should get the children away from the fighting area, but she herself did not want to go. "I'm not going to run away," she answered, decidedly. "My place is with my Chinese people, here in the danger zone. If I go to Sian they'll try to keep me there and not let me come back."

Her friends looked at her. She was terribly thin. Her

frail body shook now and again with fever. She seemed far older than a woman not yet forty, and they knew she could not really go on living the wandering life of the last few months without finally collapsing. But they dared not say so. To suggest that she was ill or tired would only make her more stubbornly determined to stay where she was.

The problem was solved when a message arrived from the Chinese general in the district. A group of Chinese soldiers were at the service she was conducting one evening and, when the congregation dispersed, a young soldier stayed behind. "I have a message for you." He passed over a paper. In it the general wrote that he was taking his army out of the district because a very strong Japanese force was due to move in and he had not enough soldiers to resist them. He wanted *Ai-wai-deh* to come with them to safety.

Gladys's face reddened with anger. "I'm certainly not going to run away, whatever the general says." She glared at the soldier. "The Japanese won't harm *me*. I've lived in towns before where they've been in occupation."

The soldier took another paper from his pocket and handed it to her. "Look at that, *Ai-wai-deh*. These are being posted all over the town."

The paper was about eight inches by ten, and Gladys could hardly believe what she saw. "One hundred dollars reward will be paid by the Japanese Army for information leading to the capture of The Small Woman, known as *Ai-wai-deh*!"

8

INTO THE MOUNTAINS

"WHO wants to go for a walk?"

Dozens of shrill voices shouted their delight. Dozens of eager olive-skinned arms waved in the air, and the excited children crowded round, demanding to know when and where they were going.

"It will be a very long walk. Right across the mountains and down to the great Yellow River. You'll get very tired before it's over."

"Shall we start now, *Ai-wai-deh*?"

"Shall we see any soldiers?"

"Are you coming with us?"

"Will it be for hours and hours?"

Gladys looked at the children thronging the dirty, rubble-filled courtyard of the Inn of Eight Happinesses. "Not for just hours and hours, but days and days. I hope we shan't see any soldiers, and we'll have to hide very quickly if we do. . . ."

". . . or else they'll kill us." The small boy who shouted did not seem very worried at the prospect. The idea of a long walk was far more exciting than any of its dangers.

"Perhaps. But I *am* coming with you. I've had to go away a lot during these last two years, but now I shall stay with you right to the end of the journey."

68

The children shouted with delight that they would have their beloved *Ai-wai-deh* to themselves for days and days, while Gladys looked at them and wondered whether they could possibly survive all the difficulties that lay ahead of them.

*   *   *

She had only just managed to get out of Tsehchow in time. Not everyone in the city was her friend, and the reward of a hundred dollars, a small fortune, would certainly have been too great a temptation to some of the Chinese who wanted both to get money and to curry favour with the Japanese. The poster announcing that she was a "wanted person" forced her to make up her mind not only to get out of Tsehchow, where she had been staying with the missionaries, but to get away altogether from the province of Shansi where she had spent all her time in China. Clearly it would soon be completely over-run by the Japanese. She hated running away, but it was more sensible to be alive, and working somewhere else, than dead or in a prison-camp in Shansi. Even so, she only just made up her mind in time. As the Japanese broke in through one of the city gates she escaped through the other, dashed for safety, hid amongst the grain-fields and was wounded by a sniper's bullet as she raced across a cemetery.

It took her two days to reach Yangcheng, into the ruins of which the population had moved back for a while from the hills. The streets were filthy, the houses almost all burned, the *yamen* no more than a shell of a building. The Mandarin, when she saw him, had discarded his beautiful robes of office for a plain, faded blue gown and trousers. But his old, lined face broke into a smile as she came into the room where he sat. She told him that she proposed to leave the province and take the children with her. He shook his head anxiously, and pointed out that taking children to Sian now would be very different from sending a hundred of them from Tsehchow, as the mission had done a little while earlier.

"You dare not go on the roads, for they're full of soldiers. Even if you find the mule-tracks over the mountains you'll have to cross through territory which the Japanese are occupying. You're almost certain to be captured somewhere on the road."

"How long will it take us?" demanded Gladys, refusing to listen to any arguments now she had made up her mind.

"It used to take the mule-trains four days. With the children you will not do it in less than twelve." He glanced at her sharply. "How many children are you taking?"

She thought of the crowd in the inn courtyard, living on whatever they could pick up. The first half-dozen had been added to again and again, though Ninepence, Less, the slave-girl Sualan and the earlier ones were still with her. She could not leave any of them behind.

"I shall take them all. There are just under a hundred!"

The Mandarin looked as if he could not believe his ears. Then he shook his head again. "*Ai-wai-deh*, you're mad. You *must* be mad. But then, you have done mad things ever since you came to Yangcheng. So I suppose you'll do this, too." He spoke very solemnly. "May God

70

protect you, *Ai-wai-deh*, and keep you on the way. I'll try and help Him a little by sending some carriers with you for the first day or so with some sacks of grain for you to live on."

*   *   *

It was to be a great deal worse than even Gladys had imagined.

The children had no real idea of how long the trek would be, and the little ones raced up and down the path, wearying themselves at the very beginning, as if they were only out for an afternoon's walk. Almost as soon as they set out they declared that they were hungry, and before long they were tired, too, and pleaded to be carried. But Gladys's real anxieties were whether they would be able to find enough food on the long trail, where they would find shelter, and what would happen if any of them fell really ill.

Food, for the first three days, was not much of a problem. The Mandarin's sacks of grain ensured that they would not starve, though some would have to be saved for later on the journey. Nor, the first night, need she worry about shelter. At dusk they arrived at a village where the Buddhist priest gazed at them in astonishment. But Chinese people are kind, friendly and hospitable, and he allowed all the hundred of them to sleep in the Buddhist temple, Christians though they were, surrounded by images and the bright little eyes of the rats that infested the old building. Not even the rats kept the children awake. Indeed, fortunately, the smaller ones seemed able to fall asleep by day or night wherever they sat down.

The second night was different. There was no priest, no village, and they had to huddle together to keep warm under the shelter of the rocks by the roadside. By morning they were almost too cold to move. Gladys did not dare to warn them that there would be worse nights ahead.

On the third day the carriers said they must return to Yangcheng, for they had reached the end of the Mandarin's territory; but fortunately a man on a mule caught up with them and offered them shelter in his village.

That seemed to be the end of their good fortune. For the next couple of days they were really in the mountains, though from time to time the tracks led downwards and joined a road for a while. The children's feet were sore, and their sandals were wearing through. They were tired but more than anything else they were hungry. And Gladys knew they could only have a little of the precious millet to eat each day, for there were many miles ahead of them before they would catch sight of the Yellow River which bounded the province of Shansi. By the fifth day they were in territory that was completely unknown to her, beyond the villages she had visited as the Mandarin's Foot Inspector. All she knew was that they must follow the tracks, on and on.

It was when they were in the middle of a gorge that one of the little boys turned from the head of the column and raced back to her, shouting.

"Soldiers, *Ai-wai-deh*! There's soldiers just round the corner of the path!"

There was no time to hide the children. All they could do was to huddle together in terror. Then, round the rocks came a group of men in bedraggled khaki uniforms, rifles across their backs. To her great relief she saw at once that they were Chinese, and no one could have been more astonished than the men themselves when they found themselves surrounded by hordes of children, ranging from five to fifteen years of age, all shouting in delight. There were long explanations, in the middle of which they had to dive for cover as Japanese planes flew overhead. Then the soldiers decided to make camp for the night where they had met. From their packs they pulled out food which they gladly shared with the children, who had never seen such wonderful things to eat in Yangcheng as long as they could remember. Under the stars they fell asleep, tired, full and content.

* * *

That night was to be the last they spent in comfort for what seemed like weeks. In fact, it was only one week, but it was the longest that Gladys could ever remember. Each day was a worse drag up and down the rough, stony paths. Each night—and they had to spend every one on the mountains amongst the rocks—seemed colder than the last. The small children were perpetually weeping with hunger and fatigue. Their feet were terribly bruised and cut. Now and again the tracks were so dangerous that they had to go hand in hand. From time to time the path disappeared altogether, and they had to scramble down the mountainside, the older ones making a human chain to pass the smaller ones to safety. Gladys hardly kept count of the days and, at last, the small voices were too tired even to sing the hymns in which she led them.

It was on the sixth night of the journey that they camped

with the soldiers, who had warned her that the Yellow River was still a great way off. They had frightened her a little, too, by saying that the Japanese were in control of much of the territory by the river. She counted off the days since the terrible trek began. Six to her meeting with the soldiers. Seven, eight, nine, ten, eleven had gone, and she almost gave up. She knew she had fever, and was probably in worse condition than the children themselves. Then, on the twelfth day, she saw what she was longing for. The hills began to break away, and soon they could see the broad plains below them. In the distance, the sun shone silver on a long streak of water.

The Yellow River was in sight.

The children cheered with delight, and questions burst out at once. "Will there be food for us?" They were already reduced to eating almost nothing at all, for the millet they had carried was gone, except for a scraping in the bottom of the sacks.

"How shall we get across the river?"

Gladys answered with all the faith in God which the years had given her. "There will be villages by the river. The people are sure to help us. And we shall go across the great river on boats. On the other side we shall be away from the Japanese, and we'll be safe!"

But, in spite of her faith, Gladys was wrong.

When they reached the river at last and found a village which she knew must be Yuan Ku it was completely deserted, except for an old man who seemed slightly mad. There was no food to be found. And, even worse, there were no boats.

"The Japanese are coming," was all the old man could

say. "The villagers have all gone, and they won't come back. They went down the river and took the boats with them." He glared maliciously at Gladys and her hundred tattered children. "You'd better go back where you came from!"

9

THE LONG, LONG TREK

FOR three days Gladys stayed disconsolately by the river-bank. She could not believe that God had allowed her to face the hardships of the past two weeks—indeed, that He had told her to take to the mountains—and would now leave her by the banks of the Yellow River to have her family destroyed by the Japanese armies. Yet, at the same time, she could see no hope of crossing the wide river. Day by day the children grew more frightened and querulous. They had scraped the very bottom of their empty sacks, and searched the houses, the streets and the garbage cans to try and find something to eat. Now, there was nothing to be found. Nor had any villagers appeared. It seemed that the old man had told the exact truth. Everyone had left. There was no means whatever of getting across the river. Yet, at the same time, it was just as hopeless to try and go back through the mountains.

* * *

"*Ai-wai-deh!* Look!"

They were sitting in a wide circle by the river, singing a hymn when one of the smaller children suddenly shouted. Following his pointing finger Gladys gazed up the river-bank. Rifle in hand, a Chinese officer was watching them. He beckoned sharply and a group of soldiers came out from the cover of the houses and moved forward, rifles trained towards them.

"Who are you?" The officer's voice was angry and suspicious. "And where do you come from? Who are these children?" Before she could answer he looked in astonishment at Gladys as she got to her feet. Though she was no taller than most Chinese women it was clear that she was a westerner. "You are a foreigner! Explain—quickly!"

He looked as if he could hardly credit her story, but the children shouted their own excited comments and he was forced to believe the incredible tale of the fortnight's trek through the mountains. "Didn't you know that this is a battle area?" he asked. "That it is forbidden to cross the Yellow River?"

As Gladys shook her head he took a whistle from his pocket and blew three sharp blasts on it. From the farther bank of the river she saw boats pushing out, manned by soldiers.

"It will need three journeys to take the children across," he told her, "and if the Japanese planes catch sight of you there is nothing anyone can do to save you. They will sink the boats, even if they are only filled with children." He looked at her in a puzzled way. "I cannot understand why the enemy planes have not been bombing the river these last three days. They've been doing it constantly until now."

Gladys told him with conviction that *she* knew why. God, who had brought them to the river, had kept them in safety while they camped there. And she was quite certain that no planes would attack them as they crossed. As the last boatload of children disembarked at the far

77

side of the Yellow River, completely unharmed, the officer could only shake his head again in astonishment. Perhaps there was something in what she had said, after all.

*　*　*

Even on the other side of the great river it was to be a long journey to Sian, and disappointment was to meet them at the end of it.

But, on the first night, there was the joy of safety, food and shelter in a friendly town. True, an officious policeman tried to arrest Gladys because she had crossed the river when it was forbidden, but that was soon put right by the Mandarin of the town. In a temple courtyard the children slept, as they had done on the first night of their journey, undisturbed and well-fed. Gladys was able to bathe their feet, tie up the cuts and sores and see them fall to sleep in peace and exhaustion. In the morning the Mandarin gave them new hope.

"You will not be able to travel the whole way to Sian," he warned Gladys. "There will be more walking for you, I'm afraid, and part of it will be what you have done before—over the mountains. But for a while, at any rate, you can travel more easily. There is a train which will take you for the next four days."

As Gladys explained it all to the children they looked puzzled. "What is a train, *Ai-wai-deh*?" asked the small ones. They were soon to find out. When Gladys demanded that every one of them should wash before they went to the station there was a concerted dash for the fountain in the temple courtyard, and they washed with more enthusiasm than they had done for weeks.

On the level ground which served for a platform they crowded in three lines. Suddenly there was a sound in the distance, and the chattering stopped. The noise grew louder, and the train appeared. To the children, seeing smoke belching from the chimney and hearing the rattle and crash of the trucks, it looked like the biggest dragon they had ever imagined. As it rushed towards them along the rails, with brakes squealing and a sharp series of blasts on the whistle, the children screamed with terror. The three lines broke and they scattered in every direction. In half a minute there was not a single one to be seen.

It took more than half an hour to get them together again, and not even their beloved *Ai-wai-deh*, at first, could persuade the smallest ones to face the station again. They had hidden in buildings, behind piles of goods, and one group of eight-year-olds had run all the way back to the temple to escape the dragon. But, at last, they were not only collected on the platform but packed into the train itself. The carriages were no more than long wooden boxes without seats, but to the children they provided the most exciting journey they had ever known.

For four days the train chugged along on its slow journey, stopping and waiting without any seeming reason, until it finally stopped altogether. The line ahead was broken. A bridge was blown up, and it could go no further. The Mandarin by the Yellow River had been right. If they were going to reach Sian they would have to walk.

* * *

The officer who had found them the boats to cross the

river had looked at Gladys with real concern, telling her she was ill and that she should see a Chinese Army doctor at the first town she came to. She had refused, saying she was quite well and must get the children to the end of the journey. But now Sualan and the rest of the older girls were themselves getting worried about her, too. She was terribly thin, her face was drawn, she easily broke into tears and there were times when she did not quite seem to know what she was saying. It was evident that only by a great effort of will had she come so far. Four days of trekking through the mountains, even Gladys herself had to admit, was almost more than she could bear to face. And yet, if they were ever to reach Sian, it must be done.

There were no enemy soldiers to worry about this time, but often the track disappeared completely and they had to cast about until they found the place where it continued. The nights were colder than ever. The children, even after the train ride, were almost completely exhausted and there was one moment when the whole company, including Gladys, simply sat down and wept until they could cry no more. That night she lay down, shivering with cold and fever, and wished she could die. Only the certainty that God would give her strength to finish the journey made her get up next morning and go on.

But at last the four days of weary wandering over the mountains came to an end. The plain spread out below them again and, lying snugly below the hills, was the town of Tung Kwan. Not even a hundred children were an astonishment to the inhabitants here, for they had seen many thousands of refugees passing through, and though food was scarce the people were prepared to go with less themselves so that others worse off might eat a little. Sian, however, was many days' journey away and, what was much worse, everyone she spoke to assured Gladys that no trains ran any longer on the railway. The Japanese were always in wait to ambush them.

*   *   *

Once more the local Mandarin came to her help. She had gone to see him, leaving most of the smaller children lying asleep in a disused temple, while the older ones sat disconsolately wondering how much longer they could go on.

"It is true that passenger trains no longer run," said the old official, "but there is *one* train that still goes occasionally."

"What is that?"

"It is a coal train to Hwa Chow. Nothing but coal wagons, no seats, no coaches. It would be very uncomfortable!"

"When does it leave?"

"To-night." The Mandarin saw the delight on Gladys's face. "I will talk to the driver. The station is only fifty yards from the temple where your children are asleep."

With the help of the older children and one or two men the dozens of smaller children were carried to the trucks, and laid amongst the lumps of coal. Older boys and girls scrambled up into each truck, to make sure the little ones did not fall out in their sleep or try to leap off, in fright, when they wakened. Then, through the night, the coal train with its strange load rattled on its way. Delighted

81   F

rather than upset to find themselves black with coal-dust when morning came, the children shouted with pleasure at the strange new landscape with its green fields and trees. The excitement of the strange journey made up for the fact that they had nothing to eat until they reached Hwa Chow. From that city another train would take them the rest of the way.

How long they were kept in the refugee-centre at Hwa Chow Gladys could never remember. Her mind was getting muddled and there were times when she hardly knew where she was. Only one thing mattered, and she kept on saying it again and again.

"I must get the children to Sian . . . to the end of the journey."

At last the day came. There was no more walking. All they had to do was crowd into the train that moved slowly across the plains to Sian. Gladys fretted at every stop and, when the train moved on again, she said the same thing over and over.

"We're nearly there. The journey's almost over."

And, at last, it *was* over. The old Chinese town, like Yangcheng only very much bigger, with high walls, huge gates and the green roofs of its innumerable temples showing above, stood before them. For weeks, ever since they had sung hymns to keep up their courage through the mountains, Gladys had promised that they should march into their dream-city, where they would be welcomed and cared for, singing one of their favourite hymns. And, indeed, forming into their usual crocodile, with the little ones at the front, they marched up to the gate. Gladys would not believe what she saw.

It was not only closed, but barred against them. From the top of the gate a watchman shouted.

"Go away, woman! The city is closed! It's full of refugees and we can't take in any more! Go away!"

10

OUT OF CHINA AT LAST

THE watchman on the wall was telling the truth. The city *was* closed to refugees. But that did not mean there was no hope for the children. The New Life Movement, which had organized the refugee work in Sian, and which had been begun by Madame Chiang Kai-Shek, had workers all through these towns and very soon some of them discovered the miserable crowd of tired and weeping children. A few questions revealed who they were and where they had come from. Gladys asked about the children who had been sent from Tsehchow.

"Oh, they're all in Fufeng, safe and well. In a little while you will be there, too."

"Do you mean we haven't got to go back over the mountains?" asked one small girl, plaintively.

The New Life Worker smiled cheerfully. "All the way to Yangcheng? No. I don't think you'd get over the river again now! There will be another journey on a train and you'll be at Fufeng. *That* city won't have closed gates, I promise you."

As it turned out she was quite right. In a day or so the whole family was at Fufeng, housed in temples, court-yards and private homes. There were cleanly-washed clothes instead of rags; feet were tenderly bathed and the sore places wrapped up; there was food for everyone, even if it wasn't the sort of food they had been accustomed to in their own province beyond the Yellow River. There were other children by the hundred, too, though none of them had the same incredible story to tell as had *Ai-wai-deh*'s noisy family. In and out of the house where Gladys was staying the children trotted all day long with news, questions and excited chatter.

* * *

But, although for the time being it was the end of the long and terrible journey for the children, it was different for the small woman who had brought them. *They* were safe; *she* suddenly felt exhausted, alone and uncertain what to do next. There were no decisions to be made, no dangers to be faced. Though she would not admit it to herself, Gladys was not only tired but ill. It was simply because she *had* to bring the children to safety that she had managed to go on so long. Then, for the time being, the problem of what to do was suddenly solved. Two simple Chinese women who were conducting Christian services in a few of the houses outside the city walls asked her to go with them and share in the preaching. Gladys was grateful for the opportunity to do something instead of sitting about thinking how tired she felt. She set off with the evangelists, reached the first house and, after they had introduced her, stood up to speak.

She opened her mouth and found she could not say anything. For a moment she stood staring at the little group of women. They seemed to spin round and round. Everything went black, and she toppled to the floor.

The next thing she knew was that she was in hospital.

For a long time she did not know who she was or where she had been. Nor did the doctors or the nurses. All they knew about her was that she had been brought to the hospital—an American Mission Hospital some distance from Fufeng, where the children were quartered—by a peasant driving a bullock-cart and left in their charge. In her delirium she talked about Yangcheng, the Mandarin, the prison, the mountains and the Japanese. And always about children—her children, she said, but to the listening nurses it seemed as if she must have scores of them. For a long time they thought she was Chinese, for she always spoke in the dialect of the Shansi province. Then, at last, she started speaking English and talking about London.

It was a very long time before she began to recover. The long, long trek over the mountains, when she had so often gone without food to make sure that the children had a little, had weakened her terribly, and she had never completely got over being beaten up by Japanese soldiers in Tsehchow. Even when she began to get better and was able to move about the hospital, helping where she could, she told the nurses and doctors very little about her adventures in bringing the children to safety.

Once she was discharged from the hospital she again found herself quite uncertain what to do. She had no money and no one to support her, for she did not belong to any missionary society. She had lived by faith and, from the moment she had set out from London to travel by the Trans-Siberian Railway to China, she had simply met each situation as it arose. She had stood up to Jeannie Lawson, to the Mandarin, to the villagers, to the Japanese.

Now, with no one to struggle against and no special dangers to be met, she felt the one thing she would like to do would be to go home. She found it funny to talk about "home". She had become a Chinese citizen so that she could share the life of the people more intimately; she did not really belong to England any more. In any case, England was at war, and even if she had had enough money—and she had none at all—it would have been impossible to travel by land or sea to the little house at Edmonton, in north London. The only thing to do, then, was to help where she could.

"Will you give us some help amongst the refugees?" asked a worker from the New Life Movement.

"Will you teach us English?" requested a couple of ambitious young policemen.

"If you can teach the police, surely you can teach us, too," suggested some of the officials at the *yamen*.

*　　*　　*

She said "yes" to each thing as it came. Every job gave her a little money to live on. There was still plenty of time to do as she liked, and in her own free time she continued preaching. As the Japanese advanced she was driven further and further west, across the plains and mountains until she was almost on the Tibetan border. Now, however, a new danger was growing. There were really two Chinese armies struggling against the Japanese and, very soon, they were to be fighting against each other once the Japanese had been beaten. The Chinese under General Chiang Kai-Shek were well-disposed towards Christianity and supported its missions, colleges and hospitals. The

87

other group was Communist and, because of this, they were opposed to everything to do with Christianity. They hated foreigners and, especially, they hated missionaries. In the end, of course, it was the Communist party which gained control of China after the Japanese had been driven out.

Away on the borders of Tibet was a town called Ching Fu, and there Gladys at last found herself working and preaching. Here the Chinese themselves were at war with each other, for the Japanese were far away, and, at last, the town fell to the Communists. Gladys was in a difficult position. If she stayed she might be imprisoned or even shot, but to escape was almost impossible, for the Communists held the country round about Ching Fu. On Christmas Day she went to church to preach for the last time, and as she went in some of the young Christians met her.

"You must escape as fast as you can. The Communists know you are here. If they capture you they'll kill you."

"I must take the service first," she insisted. So she did and then, while Communist soldiers were looking for her, she slipped out of the city gate, with her Chinese speech and dress so much like one of themselves that they did not notice her. With nothing but a basket and a Bible she set off across the hills once more to find her way to Chungking. From there it should be possible to sail down the Yangtse River to the coast.

It was not so easy as she had thought to reach the Nationalist Chinese headquarters at Chungking, for she had to take unfrequented paths over the mountains to dodge the fighting and escape the Communist patrols.

Once in Chungking, too, her dreams of getting to the coast were shattered.

"Go down the river? I'm afraid that's quite hopeless," said her friends. "There's fighting all the way down. No one would consider taking you."

Gladys found it was only too true. Every boatman refused to have anything to do with a white Christian missionary, however Chinese she sounded. Instead, she had once more to spend her time preaching. She concentrated her work on the young people and students, with whom she made friends easily wherever she went. Then, one day, a friend came to her and told her she would be able to get to the coast after all.

"Have you found a boat to take me?"

Her friend smiled gently. "Oh, no. No one can go down the river. You're going by air."

Gladys gazed in astonishment. "Me? In an aeroplane? I've never been up there in my life. I should be scared stiff." Then she thought of a new difficulty. "The fare must be enormous! I couldn't possibly afford it."

Her friend leaned forward and handed her an envelope. "You don't have to find the money. Here's your ticket. It's already been paid for."

"Paid for? Who by?" Gladys still could not believe that anyone would pay so much money to get her away from the far south of China to the coast.

"Friends who want to help you." At first it was the only answer she could get. Then, at last, she got at the truth. The young people she had been working with were determined to help her. To do so they had sold their clothes and their shoes, while the students had sold their books.

Ai-wai-deh was loved by young people wherever she went. When at last she got to the airport to board the plane two of the young people came to see her off. They were the only two who could walk there. The rest had no shoes to walk in.

*　　*　　*

Shanghai was still a long way from England, and it was one thing to have friends who would pay the fare from Chungking to Shanghai and quite another to get the money for a trip from Shanghai to London. Once more, help came in an astonishing way. She was talking to a group of Americans when a woman from Shansi passed by and Gladys, recognizing her distinctive costume, spoke to her in her own dialect. The Americans looked at her in surprise.

"Do you know Shansi Province?"

Gladys nodded, and smiled at their next question. "There was a little woman missionary up there. She brought a hundred children to safety across the mountains to Fufeng. *Ai-wai-deh*, she was called. I guess you never met her?"

"That was me," she replied simply.

The Americans gaped at her. "Why, ma'am, you don't look big enough to walk up one mountain, never mind doing all the things they say you did. How long have you been in China?"

"Seventeen years."

"Why, that's half a lifetime! Don't you ever want to go home?"

"China is my home, I suppose. Though I'm not sure

what will happen to me if the Communists come to power, even though I am a nationalized Chinese subject." She nodded thoughtfully. "It would be nice to see England again, though. I'd like to see my people." She brightened up and spoke crisply. "But then, what's the good of saying that? I haven't any money. I never *have* had any, and I'm not likely to, either."

It was the meeting with the Shansi woman which started things off. Although Gladys had no money of her own, and she would certainly not have dreamed of asking for anything for herself, the Americans had some spare money in a fund meant to help send German missionaries and other refugees back to their own country. The Germans had been repatriated and there was still some of the fund left.

"We could send someone else home with it, couldn't we?" the American asked his wife. "Even if she isn't a refugee and doesn't want to go to Germany?"

So it was that, three years after she had met the kindly American, Gladys Aylward was put on another plane, this time for England. In 1950, *Ai-wai-deh* came back to her old home in Edmonton, wearing a dress that was long out of fashion and carrying a Chinese Bible. She had been in China for twenty years.

11

FORMOSA

IT was a brief newspaper paragraph which sent a B.B.C. producer to see her, but at first Gladys Aylward assured him that she had no story worth telling. She really meant it, too. "Nothing very unusual ever happened to me," she assured him. "Except that I once took about a hundred children across the mountains."

Alan Burgess from the B.B.C. sat up sharply. "Tell me about it," he invited her.

From that interview came a story that was produced in a radio-series called *The Undefeated*. "Gladys Aylward" became a name known to millions of listeners. Then Alan Burgess wrote her story in a book called *The Small Woman** and tens of thousands more people heard of her. The book was made into a film and seen by millions more. Hundreds of invitations came flooding into Gladys's home, asking her to go and preach, lecture and speak about her work. To her great astonishment the "small woman" found herself famous.

By this time, however, she was busy once more. Naturally, she kept in touch, as far as she could, with the children whom she had brought out of Yangcheng. Inevitably, back in England, she tried to help her Chinese

* This present book owes a great deal to *The Small Woman*, by Alan Burgess, published by Evans Ltd.

people, too. In London she did what she could for Chinese students and nurses who came to England from Singapore and Hong Kong. In Liverpool she shared in opening a hostel for Chinese seamen and others who needed a temporary home. Then, just as surely as He had called her all those years before when she was a parlourmaid to the great explorer, she felt certain that God was speaking to her again. One word kept ringing in her mind.

"Formosa! You must go to Formosa!"

After the Japanese had been driven out of China, the Communists finally gained control of the country. Hundreds of thousands, and finally millions, of Chinese who felt they could not live under Communist rule, fled from the mainland. Some went to Hong Kong, others to Singapore. Most of the refugees, however, found their way to the big Chinese island of Formosa, not far from the mainland of China, where General Chiang Kai-Shek had set up the headquarters of his Nationalist, anti-Communist government. Missionaries had been expelled from the mainland and some had transferred to Formosa. It was not surprising that Gladys herself felt called to go back to the East and join her own Chinese people once more.

* * *

Except for an occasional visit to England to speak about her work it is in Formosa that she will be found to-day. It was a happy thing to be a missionary once more amongst the Chinese people she loved, and to be known again as *Ai-wai-deh*, rather than Miss Aylward. But, best of all, she is "Mother" to a growing family of new children as well as to all her old ones.

93

Letters flowed in from her old family. They were all grown up now. For some, the war had brought tragedy. The boy Less, the second child to come to her in Yang-cheng, brought home by Ninepence, had been shot by the Communists. But Ninepence herself, her very first child, was married with a family of her own. Another boy is an officer in the Chinese Air Force. Michael is an ordained minister in Hong Kong. Others became students, teachers, nurses, clerks. They were scattered all over the place. Some, however, were already in Formosa or came to join her there.

At Taipeh, in Formosa, you will find Gladys Aylward surrounded by a crowd of children and babies; for, once more, she is mothering the families nobody else wants to keep. It is not an inn, now, that she keeps but a proper orphanage which bears her own name—the Gladys Aylward Orphanage. Money is not quite so much of a problem because she is so well known in Britain and funds are sent out to her to help her work. Yet there is always more to do than she is able to find money or time for. A Babies' Home as well as an Orphanage is quite essential because so many of the children who come to her are no more than babies. Two of her Chinese children, John and Pauline, with three children of their own, are in charge of the Orphanage and hardly a week or two passes without one of them coming to her with the same story.

"*Ai-wai-deh*, there is a man who wants to sell us his two children."

"There was another baby left on the doorstep during the night."

94

"A woman came in and put her baby on the mat and went away. She said she had no money to keep it."

As long as Gladys Aylward is able to work there will be people who come to her with their children. As long as she is able to speak there will be people who will listen to her wonderful stories about the way in which God helps those who trust in Him. Anyone going to Formosa to look for her would naturally go to Taipeh. And anyone, seeing a tiny woman in Chinese costume surrounded by a crowd of romping children and small babies, would be almost certain to guess rightly.

"That must be *Ai-wai-deh*!"